MORGAN LONGFORD

CATCHING DUSK
WITH OUR TEETH

Sparklefoot Collective
PUBLISHING

For permission requests, email the author at: morgan.longford@gmail.com

www.morganlongford.com

ISBN: 979-8-9881220-3-6

First Printing, 2023

Morgan Longford is 43. She lives in Austin, Texas.

To Megan:

For guidance,
for believing in my greatness,
and for convincing me to believe in it too.
This book exists for you, and because of you.
(And because of a bunch of shitty dudes, tbh.)

Let's get together and talk about the modern age. - Rilo Kiley

CONTENTS

CONTENTS

Fall

CATCHING DUSK WITH OUR TEETH

WINTER

Winter walked in
wearing leather coats,
tasteful and dangerous

running a finger along the
soft spot under our jaws
sexy and cool
and fucking cold to the touch.

Pulling memories through our skin
and our teeth and our breath
catching in our throats
in terror and shame.

In panicked breaths we followed still
outside
our fears visible in clouds with
each and every
exhale.

DECEMBER

_____

"Hola" she replies,
in a
half-whisper and
half-interested

a word she has spoken
from her porch
more days than she
cares to admit.

Her age on display
in wrinkles-
deep and tan,
but soft, not leathery;

a face that has watched
mornings arrive here
from her stoop
for decades

but because its **D**ecember
and close to Christmas,
she follows with
"Feliz Navidad,"

still only in a half-whisper
still only half-interested,
from her chair,
her version of festive.

JANUARY

And here we are.
365 days from our next new
Beginning.

Promising ourselves this time
THIS TIME
we will honor the ships in our harbor.
We will eat better and sleep longer
and lose 10 and start that thing that will
make us whole.

We will learn how to read so we are
no longer
illiterate in emotional regulation.
We will hold our tongues captive.
We won't be so sensitive.

Every morning,
promising that today will be different and
I will do all the things I set sail to do
and I won't let the tide take away my
Progress.

My therapist says,
Progress not perfection
but the tides laugh and rise and
wash away what looked like growth
so I sit here again,
waiting for January
before January is done.

because it means I have a chance
to start all over again on that first day
The FIRST day
instead of just trying again tomorrow.
because how bad can it get
when we've made it this far?

FEBRUARY

Fickle, fickle February
your pleated movements
down from the North,
   in from the West,
      up from the South
Your moon in Leo.

Thirty-nine years of
     February
pushing and pulling-
    a love
      a lover-
finding reasons to stay and
selling reasons to go
but it was always negotiable.

February I'd wrap you in
leopard fur coats
as your obligations
whispered their rules.
Whispered to

Echoes to
     Shouts to
Silence.

To a place of
understanding,
defiant and deferent.
    February.
      The guardian of
the seasons.

SPRING

And every new **S**pring
as the leaves take
their branches back
and their complexions
glow in shades of green
we touch the ground
with our knees,
reach out our arms,
and cup our hands to drink
from a well of hope

Hopeful that courage will
flow through our bodies so we can
unclench our fists and
tame our butterflies and
dance ahead with our arms
open wide.

Hopeful that we will
find that golden light that
lives inside the belly of
our own man-made beasts
and that we can finally
let go of what was,
knowing that the future
knows our names.

MARCH

You marched in
unranked, defile,
in exile from your childhood.
No fanfare, no flourish,
your arrival in
unassuming worn-out Vans
silent and gradual and then
suddenly.
Your exit was the same
and still you
marched.

To the beat of
your own eyes

(deep-set, Hungarian,
wild and dark)

marched.

To the beat of your
grandfather's nose

(which adorns your face with
generations of
broken sails
and bottomless boats)

marched.

To the day of your birth
March
to your forgotten fathers of your
mother's
first, second, fifth loves and
to waiting too long
to
poem after poem you
pumped into your arms
to the poem on your
wrist.

And still you marched on
your destruction playing
in your shadows.

I tried to keep up with you,
to catch you, to make friends
with your secrets,
because I wanted to play
in the shadows too.

APRIL

Catching dusk with our teeth,
we claimed **A**pril as our own.

as We
laid on our backs
languid in youth
fervent in self-importance.
The trampoline sagged beneath us
with
the weight of our choices,
our words in our pockets.

lacking nothing and knowing everything
except that:

18 species of fireflies
exist in California and they flicker so dimly
we didn't know they were there.

Except:
what would happen tomorrow.

Except:
what would happen the next day
or years later when
vows were made in haste and
broken

broken in
hopefulness and
desperation and
selfishness;
broken. in.

we caught April in our teeth
before we watched from afar.

MAY

Inaccurate
the memories linger
longer
than
they
should.

Etched into
gray matter,
held captive by neurons,
to be rediscovered
during
May drives and
Texas thunderstorms.

Nestled deeply
under layers,
a shadow,
you are an artifact
in a thrift store flannel
unwashed and
fucking perfect.

But
you are old Austin,
man.

In an act of solidarity
with my attempts to forget,
the universe tried to
hide you,
buried you in the folds,
burnt that shit down.
literally.

burned the coffee shop I
found you in
when you learned I liked my coffee
not. too. hot.

burned the dancehall
where we didn't dance
but I dreamed of it in tune to
the jukebox

but where we sat on shaky
barstools
day drinking

shuttered the
all night diner where
you told me who you were-
the outlaw
turned hero
turned turncoat

the cafe-
closed.

The house-
sold.

All of it gone
and yet
you remain
like a relic that serves
no purpose.

SUMMER

Sweltering in our failures,
our sins
glistened in **S**ummer waves
like sweat on our bodies,

the sins of my mother
now living in me,
a scarlet letter
that she left for me
along with her
lower-case g goodbye.

A scarlet letter
once worn under clothes
but now spoken in pernicious
words.

JUNE

The men in suits came-
they knocked on our doors,
uninvited,
yet we answered uneasily,
out of courtesy.

(We didn't ask for company.)

The men in suits came-
with their gold cuff links
and veneer smiles,
and they explained to us that
they were there to help.

(We didn't need help.)

The men in suits came-
they stood on our porches and
admired our June lawns,
they told us that they were there
to protect us.

(We didn't need protecting.)

The men in suits came-
with their insincere platitudes,
pushed us aside and
entered our homes, assured us:
"we know better what you need than you do."

(We already knew what we needed.)

We watched.

We watched the men in suits
through our front windows,
the sun of the summer solstice
on our backs,
watched as they disassembled
our homes and our histories.

We watched through the windows
because the men in suits
had locked us out.
We watched through the windows
because we no longer had
a choice.

JULY

I stand now
with my back
to July,
the truth,
still warm to the
touch.

I am my father's
     father's
        daughter.
Third generation
gypsy girl.

The blood of
a traveling merchant
marine
passed on to a son
  and then to a
       daughter.

Just one.
The recessive gene.

Following in
dusty footprints
marred with
abandonment,
committed until the
edge of
discomfort.
Hopeless romantics,
but too lazy to try,

protest signs made of
white picket fences,

afraid of normal,
of status quo,
and our own
capacity for love.

I am my father's
daughter.

AUGUST

My dreams knew
what I wanted before
I even knew
what to ask.

In those moments
between
sleep and awake,
they murmur truths.

Lingering.

Radiating like
heat waves in
the middle of
August.

Listen,
they say,

Then speak.

FALL

I don't know foreign languages
but I do know how
to give up without a fight
And I know that
the Fall equinox shakes hands
with my birthday,
the day and night equal lengths,
giving me a gift of balance
year after year
if I would just
take it.

SEPTEMBER

Wipe the sapphires
from your eyes, Darling.

You are more than your scars,
and

Jeweled handcuffs don't
make you less of a prisoner.

You've bathed in **S**eptember
waves of Sadness too long.

Start turning away from
turning away.

You. Are. Limitless.

OCTOBER

October it
swallowed me whole

washed in
white
a glow from
within.

Time lost
in the belly
of a full moon
but wrapped
in the warm and
erratic
breaths of
newness.

Emerging with gold
inside,
arms open wide

my belly full
with the light of
a thousand stars.

NOVEMBER

---

for what it's worth
and whatever it means for
modern
man-
it is harvest season.

the leaves have
changed and
fallen,
returning earth to earth to
start again

And as November
becomes bare
I'm trying to remain
facing
forward

to gather to give thanks
in new boots and
winter coats
to be grateful to keep
it hidden

the rage that flows
like white blood cells
rage that, in the right light,
you can see it ripple
under the surface

escaping in breaths
from pores and
words spoken
unable to be
retrieved.

Thankful that for
today,
it is silent;
thankful that I am learning
to tame it.

CENTAUR

_____

The summers of our
discontent
swaggered itself into
Fall,
left unchecked
into winter
and now,
all the horoscopes say

it's time to let go.

Something about
eclipses and a centaur
and it's just so hard but
who am I to
tell the stars they are wrong?
And still, songs of
Maybe in spring
echo in moonbeams.

Place my heart on your chest,
You asked.

Morgan Longford is a California girl with a New York heart currently living in Texas. This is her first published collection of poetry. Morgan is also the author of *Annie the Adventurer,* as well as many short stories and essays, and has several memoirs and novels in the works. She would like if you bought all her books so that she could write full time from some coastal town some-where in the world. Her husband, son, and dog would like that as well.

As far as thank you's go, every book that has ever been born came from myriad ideas, people, experiences, feelings, spaces and places. I may have put the words to paper, but this wasn't written alone. It is a collective effort between myself and all the things above. So, I give my heartfelt thanks to: Costa Rica, Wild-flowers, The D in Detroit, Pancake, Roe, The Cosmos and The Planets and The Stars and the people that made me. Megan, ten minutes to downtown is ten minutes too far. Thank you for being the catalyst for this collection. Also, there is no such thing as too many matching tattoos, either, for anyone that is wonder-ing.

Other books and publications by Morgan Longford:

Annie the Adventurer
(Available in paperback, hardcover and ebook)
Sparklefoot Collective Publishing

Weekly publications on Substack, written under
"Pink Donut Boxes."

Featured in Sunday Mornings at the River, Poetry Diary, 2024
Available on Amazon in paperback and hardcover
Independently published

COMING SOON:

From The Treehouse Looking Out, A Memoir
Sparklefoot Collective Publishing

Three additional works coming in 2024, currently untitled.

www.ingramcontent.com/pod-product-compliance
Lightning Source LLC
Chambersburg PA
CBHW030527130626
46549CB00007B/3131